KT-472-463

图书在版编目(ＣＩＰ)数据

"明十三陵"画册：中、英、日文对照/魏玉清撰稿；朱力等
摄影．－北京：中国旅游出版社,1993.7(1995.6 重印)
ISBN 7－5032－0802－3

Ⅰ.明… Ⅱ.①魏… ②朱… Ⅲ.十三陵－摄影集 Ⅳ.
K928.76－64

中国版本图书馆 CIP 数据核字(95)第 06771 号

中国旅游出版社　　　　　　　　　　编
北京华天旅游国际广告公司　　　　　承制
中国旅游出版社　　　　　　　　　　发行
1993 年第一版 1996 年第四次印刷
书号 ISBN 7—5032—0802—3/ G·228
　　000004500
Published by China Travel & Tourism Press
A9 Jianguomennei Dajie
First Editon & First Print in 1993

THE MING TOMBS

明の十三陵

10/4
P £3-80

前　言
PREFACE
前　書　き

　　在中国的封建史上,明王朝(公元1368—1644年)是一个很重要的历史时期。明成祖朱棣在南京即位不久,出于巩固北方疆域的考虑,决定迁都北京。在营造北京宫阙城池的同时,又在昌平县境大兴土木予建陵寝。此后,由于嗣皇帝相继在其左右建陵,遂使陵区不断扩大,设施也不断完善,终于形成一个占地面积约四十平方公里的陵寝禁区。

　　明正统年间(公元1436—1450年),虽有朝臣提出过将京师迁回南京的动议,但"祖宗陵寝在兹"的现实,使"南迁"之举终不得行。此后的二百多年里,每当蒙古或女眞等部族乘秋高马壮之机,越过关隘,绕过卫所进入平原与明军对峙时,朝庭则每每以"南卫京师,北护陵寝"相号召,动员全国各地的军吏兵民到京"勤王"。祖宗陵寝实际上又是朱明王朝社稷江山的重要象征之一。

　　明朝先后有十三个皇帝的陵寝建在昌平县境的天寿山陵区。后世遂称其地日明十三陵。其实,在陵区范围内,另外还建有妃子及妃子合葬墓六处,皇子合葬墓一处。其他附属建筑如行宫,斋房,拂尘殿,祀祭署,宰牲亭,神宫监,神厨库,神马房,果园榛厂等则遍布陵区。当时还有仙人洞,九龙池,圣迹亭等名胜点缀其间。加之陵区内古木参天,流水潺潺。这一天造地设的胜景,不仅使宫庭式建筑格局的帝后陵寝更加庄严穆肃,同时也不失古典园林清幽雅素的风格,处处显示出古代建筑大师的独具匠心。

The Ming Dynasty, which lasted from A.D. 1368 to 1644, is a very important historical period in the Chinese feudal history. Soon after he succeeded to the throne in Nanjing, Ming Chengzu Zhu Di decided to move the capital to Beijing, with the consideration of strengthening the northern frontier. At the same time when the Imperial Palace was constructed in Beijing, he also had his tomb built in Changping County in the northern outskirts of Beijing. Later, all his successors followed his example and had their tombs built around his, and therefore, the tomb area had constantly been expanded and the installations in it had gradually been perfected. Finally, it became a forbidden tomb ground covering an area of 40 square kilometres as you can see today.

Later, during the Zhengtong reign (A.D. 1436--1450), some courtiers suggested that the capital be moved back to Nanjing, yet this motion was not adopted since the ancestral tombs were here in Beijing. For the 200 years afterwards, whenever Monggol and Nuzhen tribes (ancient minority nationalities in China) crossed over the mountains and confronted with the Ming army, the imperial government would call on the whole nation to come to Beijing to escort the emperor, its slogan being "defending the imperial capital in the south and safeguarding the tombs in the north". The ancestral tombs, in fact, are one of the important symbols for the Ming Dynasty.

Thirteen Ming emperors' tombs, now called the Ming Tombs, were built here at the foot of Tianshou Mountains, Changping County. Actually, in the imperial cemetery there are also 6 tombs built for concubines and one for princes. Other subsidiary buildings that can be found everywhere in the necropolis are Xinggong (a temporary dwelling place for the emperor when away from the capital), Zhaifang (Abstinence House), Fuchendian (Hall of Horsetail Whisk), Sijishu (Sacrificing Office), Zaishengting (butchering Pavilion), Shengongjian (Holy Imperial Office), Shenchuku (Holy Kitchen where sacrifices were stored) and orchards. At that time, the tomb complex was also embelished with scenic spots such as Immortals' Cave, Nine-dragon Pond, and Sage Pavilion, etc. Covered with ancient pine and cypress trees, this heavenly historical site makes the imperial tombs filled with a solemn and respectful atmosphere, yet, without losing the quiet and elegant style of the classical garden, showing everywhere the ingenuity of ancient architects.

中国封建史上、明朝（西暦1363－1644年）は一つの重要な時期であった。明朝第三代の明成祖朱棣(永楽皇帝）は、南京で即位したが、間もなく北方の守りを固めるため、北京への遷都を決定した。北京城の築城を進めると同時に、昌平県内では自らの陵墓を造営した。後の皇帝もこれに従い、次次にこの付近に陵墓を造営したため、陵区は拡大し、施設も次第に整っていった。やがて陵墓を中心とする立入禁止区域は約40k㎡にも達した。

正統年間（1436～1450年）には、朝廷内で都を再び南京に戻そうという議論が出されたが、「父祖の陵寝ここにあり」という現実により「南遷」は実現しなかった。その後200年余りモンゴル、女真などの北方民族は秋になり戦いに適した季節になると、険要の地を越え、見張りを避けて、平原に入りこんだ。こうして、明軍と対峙する度に、朝廷は「南は都を守り、北は陵寝を渡すべからず」と呼びかけ、全国から軍人、官吏や民衆を動員し、守りにあたらせた。この陵墓群はとりもなおさず明王朝の天下を示す重要な象徴でもあったのだ。

明朝の13代の皇帝が相次いでこの昌平県天寿山付近に造営されたため、ここは「明の十三陵」と呼ばれるようになった。実際には、この陵区内には、妃やその合葬墓が6基、皇子の合葬墓も一基あり、他に、行宮、斎房、払塵殿、祀祭署、宰牲亭、神宮監、神厨庫、神馬房、果園榛丁などが分布している。また、当時は仙人洞、九龍池、聖跡亭などの名勝も散在していた。

目　录
CONTENTS
目　次

神路

The Sacred Way

神 路

大宫门是进入陵区的门户,大宫门后的这条大道叫神路。它起于石牌坊,穿过大宫门,一直通向长陵,原为长陵而筑,但后来便成了全陵区的主要陵道了。该道纵贯陵园南北,全长七公里,沿线设有一系列建筑物,错落有致,极为壮观。其中又尤以石像生引人注目。

陵前神道两侧竖石像生,是皇帝生前朝会或大典、出巡时所设仪卫的象征。

明十三陵的神道石像生始建于正统元年(公元 1436 年)。三年后才将石料备齐,而精雕细刻的最终完工理应更晚一些。嘉靖十五年(公元 1536 年),世宗予建寿宫的同时,曾传旨将石像生嵾以石台,时至今日。石雕像基本完好,是一组很有价值的石雕艺术品。

The big Red Gate is the gateway to the site of the tombs. Starting from the Stone Memorial Arch, the Sacred Way passes through the Big Red Gate and leads directly to Changling. It was originally built for Changling, but later it served as the principal passageway to the entire site. Being 7 kilometres in lengh, it runs through the cemetery from north to south. Along the road stand a series of stone structures which are well arranged and most magnificent. Among them the human stone figures are most noticeable to the tourists.

The human stone figures standing on both sides of the Sacret Way are the symbols of the guards who were placed when the emperor received high officials, held grand ceremonies and went on tours.

These human stone figures were erected in 1436. It took 3 years to get the stone materials ready, and of course, it took much longer time to finish the work of carving. After 500 years, these valuable stone sculptures of art are still in fairly good condition.

大宮門は陵区に入る玄関である。大宮門の後ろのこの道は神路と呼ばれている。神路は石碑坊から始まり、大宮門をくぐって、長陵までつながる。もともと長陵のために造られたが、いつのまにか全陵区の主な陵道になった。この道は、陵園を南北に貫いて、全長7kmある。その沿線には、一連の建物が建てられている。それぞれに特徴を持ち、全体としては、きわめて壮観である。その中でも石獣、石人が人の目を引く。

陵前の神路の両側に立っている石獣、石人は、皇帝の生前、大臣が皇帝に謁見する時、または重要な式典、行幸の時の儀仗のしるしである。

明の十三陵の神路石獣、石人は正統元年(1436年)に造営が開始されたが、石材を揃えるのに三年を費やし、精細な彫刻が最終的に完成したのは、もっと遅い。嘉靖十五年(1536年)、世宗が寿宮を建てる折りに、石獣、石人に石台をつけよと命じたので、今日まで、石彫刻像はほぼ完璧に残っている。そのため、非常に価値の高い石彫刻芸術品になっている。

石牌坊 　建于嘉靖十九年（公元 1540 年），五门六柱十一楼，是世宗皇帝为颂扬祖宗的业绩建造的。石雕纹饰精美，建筑结构严谨。

Stone Memorial Arch 　The stone Memorial Arch, built of white marble, was erected in Jiajing Shijiunian (A.D.1540). It has six pillars, five doors, and eleven sections. It is exquisitely carved with designs of animals and other things on the pillars.

石牌坊 　嘉靖十九年（1540年）に建てられ、それは世宗皇帝が父祖の功績をほめたたえるために造られ たものである。石の彫刻は美しく、また精密であり、建 物の組み立て方が、しっかりしている。

神路

The Sacred Way

神路

大宫门 大宫门是进入陵区的门户,门前两侧立有下马碑,举行陵祭时,上至皇帝,下至各级官员,都要在门外落轿,下马,步入陵区,以示崇敬。

The Big Red Gate   The big Red Gate is the gateway to the tomb complex, and in front of it stands the Dismounting Stele, one on each side. When sacrifices were held, all the officials including the emperor had to dismount from Sedan or horseback in front of the gate and then walk to the tomb site in order to show their respects to their ancestors.

大宮門   大宮門は、陵区に入る玄関で、門前の両側に下馬碑が立てられている。陵祭が行なわれる時は、皇帝から、下の各階級の役人まで、門外でかごや馬から降り、歩いて陵区に入ることになっている。その事で、崇敬の気持を示すのである。

神功圣德碑碑亭 建筑平面呈方形,内竖一石碑,刻有仁宗皇帝叙述其父皇一生功德的碑文三千余字。碑阴、碑侧则有清朝皇帝的巡陵诗文。

Pavilion of Divine Merit and Sagely Virtue Stele   The structure is square in shape, with a stone stele standing inside on which were inscribed more than 3,000 words composed by Emperor Ren Zong. The back and the side of the stele were inscribed with verses by emperors of the Qing Dynasty while touring the Ming tombs.

神功聖徳碑碑亭   建物は正方形で、中に一つの石碑が立てられている。その上に仁宗皇帝が父の生涯の功績を称えた碑文三千字余りが刻まれている。碑の後ろと横には、清朝皇帝の巡陵詩文が彫られている。

文臣

Civilian Officials

文官

勳臣

Ministers of Merit

勛官

武臣

Military Officers

武官

马

Stone Horse

馬

麒麟

Stone Qiling or Unicon

麒麟

华表

White Marble Column

華表

獅子
———
Stone Lion
———
獅子

骆驼
———
Stone Camel
———
骆驼

象

Stone Elephant

象

獬豸　獬豸是传说中的独角兽，能明辨是非。明朝掌管风纪法度的官员叫"风宪官"，其帽饰即用獬豸。

Stone Xiezhi (mythical beast)　Xiezhi was a mythical beast of the feline family which was said to be able to distinguish between right and wrong. In the Ming Dynasty, an official in charge of disciplines and laws was called "discipline and law official" whose headgear had the design of Xiezhi.

獬豸（カイチ）　獬豸は、伝説上、角が一つしかなく、善悪の判断できる動物である。明朝の風紀や法律を管理する役人を「風憲官」と呼ばれていた。風憲官の帽子の飾りは獬豸であった。

龙凤门　造型别致，建立在石像生群的末端。

Longfeng Gate (Gate with Dragon and Phoenix Design)　Uniquely-shaped, the Longfeng Gate stands at the end of Stone figures.

龍鳳門　型がユニークで、立ち並んだ石獣、石人の一番端に建てられている。

長陵

Changling

長　陵

長陵,是明成祖朱棣与其皇后徐氏的合葬陵寝。始建于永乐七年（公元 1409 年）五月,作为地面主要建筑的祾恩殿则建成于宣德二年（公元 1427 年）三月。

朱棣（公元 1360——1424 年）,明太祖朱元璋第四子。初封燕王,"靖难之役"后即位称帝。在位二十二年,病死于出征漠北班师回京的路上,终年六十五岁。

皇后徐氏,明朝开国元勋中山王徐达的长女,初封燕王妃,永乐五年,四十六岁病逝于南京。永乐十一年（公元 1413 年）迁葬北京,与朱棣合葬于长陵。

Changling is the tomb for Zhu Di, Emperor Yong Le, the third Ming emperor, and his wife Empress Xu. The tomb was constructed in May 1409. Ling'endian (Hall of Prominent Favour), the principal ground structure was built in March 1427.

Zhu Di (1360——1424) was the fourth son of Zhu Yuanzhang, the first emperor of the Ming Dynasty. He was initially made Prince Yan, and later became the third emperor after putting down the civil strife known as "Jingnanzhiyi" in the Chinese history. He ruled for 22 years and died of illness at the age of 65.

His wife Empress Xu, the eldest daughter of Xu Da who was one of the founders of the Ming Dynasty, was initially made Princess Yan. She died of illness in Nanjing in 1407 when she was 46. In 1413, her remains were transferred to Beijing and later buried in the tomb of Changling together with Emperor Zhu Di.

長陵は明成祖朱棣（永楽皇帝）と皇后徐氏の合葬陵寝で、永楽七年（1409年）五月に造営されたものである。地上にある重要な建物である祾恩殿は宣徳二年（1427年）三月に建てられたのである。

朱棣（1360－1424年）は明太祖朱元璋の第四子である。最初は燕王に封ぜられ、「靖難戦争」のあと、皇帝に即位し、帝と称した。二十二年間帝位についていたが、漠北へ遠征し、北京に帰る途中で崩御し、享年六十五歳であった。

皇后徐氏は、明朝開国の元勲中山王徐達の長女で、最初は燕王妃に封ぜられ、永楽五年四十六歳の時、南京で病死した。永楽十一年（1413年）北京に改葬され、その後また朱棣と長陵に合葬された。

长陵鸟瞰

A Bird's Eye View of Changling

長陵の鳥瞰図

长陵明楼

Minglou (Soul Tower) of Changling

長陵の明楼

长陵秋色

Changling in Fall

長陵の秋色

焚帛炉

Silk Burner

焚帛炉

长陵祾恩殿外景　长陵祾恩殿面阔九间,进深五间,占地四千多平米。建成于宣德二年(公元 1427 年),至今保存完好。

The Exterior of Ling'endian　Ling'endian, built in Xuande Ernian (A.D.1427), covers an area of more than 4,000 square metres, 9 rooms in length and 5 rooms in breadth, and is still well preserved.

長陵祾恩殿の外景　長陵の祾恩殿は、横幅九間（正面の柱間数を言う）、奥行き五間で、敷地面積は4000㎡余りある。宣徳二年（1427年）に建てられたもので、今日まで程ど完全な形で保存されている。

十三陵长陵

The Tomb of Changling at the Ming Tombs

十三陵の長陵

长陵祾恩殿内景　殿内面积 1956
平方米，十六根楠木柱子，有的高达十
三米以上，胸径都在一米左右，不加任
何修饰，朴实无华，古色古香。

The Interior of Ling'endian (Hall
of Prominent Favour)　The hall,
covering a total floor space of 1956
square metres, is supported by 16 huge
pillars of nanmu (a special kind of
hardwood), 13 metres in height and
about 1 metre in diameter. These pillars
are all made of natural, unpainted
wood without any decorations.

長陵祾恩殿内部　殿内面積1956
㎡で、十六本のクスノキの柱があり、
高いもので13m以上にも達している。
幹の直径は１mぐらいあり、何も飾り
気がなく、実に簡素で、色や香りから
昔の雰囲気をかもし出している。

长陵五供

Five Kinds of Offerings in Changling

長陵五供（五種類の祭祀用具）

长陵宝顶

The Emperor's Grave Mound of Changling

長陵の宝頂

鼍龙碑亭

Pavilion of Stone Alligator Stele

鼉龍碑亭

献 陵

Xianling

献 陵

献陵，是仁宗皇帝朱高炽的陵寝，建于公元 1426 年。

朱高炽（公元 1378—1425 年），系成祖朱棣嫡长子。生于凤阳，十八岁时召至南京，永乐二年二十七岁时册立为皇太子。二十二年（公元 1424 年）七月，其父皇病逝于榆木川，同年的八月十五日朱高炽即位称帝。第二年五月病死于皇宫钦安殿。在位不足九个月，终年四十八岁。

皇后张氏，永城人，初封燕世子妃，皇太子妃，仁宗即位，进封皇后。正统七年（公元 1442 年）十月去世，与仁宗合葬献陵。

Xianling, the tomb for Zhu Gaochi, Emperor Ren Zong, was built in 1426.

Zhu Gaochi (1378—1425) was the eldest son of Emperor Zhu Di. Born in Fengyang, he was called to Nanjing at the age of 18. In 1404, when he was 27, his father died of illness in Yumuchuan (present Duolun County in Inner Mongolia). On August 15 of the same year, Zhu Gaochi succeeded to the throne and became an emperor. In May of the following year, he died of illness in Qin'andian of the imperial palace. He was 48 when he died and had been an emperor for less than 9 months.

His wife Empress Zhang from Yongcheng (present Kaifeng in Henan) was first raised to the rank of concubine, then Crown Princess, and finally became the empress when Ren Zong succeeded to the throne. She died in October 1442, and was buried in Xianling with Emperor Ren Zong.

献陵は仁宗皇帝朱高熾（洪熙帝）の陵寝で、1426年に造営されたのである。

朱高熾（1378－1425年）は成祖朱棣の長男で、鳳陽で生まれ、十八歳の時、南京に呼び寄せられ、永楽二年二十七歳で皇太子に冊立された。永楽二十二年（1424年）七月、父親が榆木川で病歿し、同年の八月十五日朱高熾が即位した。翌年五月皇居の欽安殿で病歿し、在位はわずか九ヶ月で、享年四十八歳であった。

献陵陵园

Xianling Necropolis

献陵の陵園

春到献陵

Xianling in Spring

春の献陵

献陵 献陵的建造,因山势所限,分为前后两组建筑。前部分建陵门,祾恩殿自成一院落,后一院落则由三座门起始,由二柱门、石供案、明楼、宝城等组成。

The Tomb of Xianling Beijing restricted by the surrounding mountains, the structures of Xianling are devided into two parts: the front part and the rear part. The front part is made up of Xianling Gate and Ling'endian, the latter looking virtually like a natural courtyard. The rear part starting from Sanzuomen (Triple Gates) is composed of Erzhumen (Two-pillar Gate), Stone Offering Table, Minlou and Baocheng (Precious Citadel).

献陵 献陵は山の地勢により、建物は二つの部分に分かれている。前の部分は陵門で、祾殿は独立した一つの庭になっている。後ろの部分は、三座門をはじめ、二柱門、石供案、明楼と宝城からなっている。

景 陵

Jingling

景　陵

景陵是宣宗皇帝朱瞻基与继后孙氏的合葬陵。建于公元 1435 年。

朱瞻基（公元 1399——1435 年），仁宗长子。生于北京，十一岁时立为皇太孙。洪熙元年（公元 1425 年）六月即皇帝位。在位十年，三十八岁病逝乾清宫。

原配皇后胡氏，以"无子且病"为辞，退居长安宫，贵妃孙氏继封为皇后。天顺六年（公元 1462 年）九月病卒。同年十一月合葬景陵。

Built in 1435, Jingling is the tomb for Zhu Zhanji, Emperor Xuan Zong and his second wife Empress Sun.

Zhu Zhanji (1399--1435), the eldest son of Emperor Ren Zong, was born in Beijing. He was made the successor to Crown Prince when he was 11. He Succeeded to the throne in June 1420, and had been on the throne for 10 years. He died of illness in Qianqinggong (Palace of Celestial Purity) at the age of 38.

Honourable Imperial Concubine Sun became the empress after Emperor Xuan Zong's first wife Empress Hu withdrew from the rank of empress because of childless and eye disease and lived in Chang'angong since then. Empress Sun died of illness in September 1462 and was buried in Jingling in November of the same year.

景陵は宣宗皇帝朱瞻基（宣徳皇帝）と後妻孫氏の合葬陵で、1435年に建てられたのである。

朱瞻基（1399−1435年）は仁宗の長男で、北京で生まれ、十一歳の時皇太孫に冊立された。洪熙元年（1425年）六月に即位したが、在位十年で、三十八歳の時乾清宮で病歿した。

朱瞻基の最初の皇后胡氏は「無子目病」という理由で、長安宮に隠居したため、貴妃孫氏が皇后に封ぜられた。孫氏が天順六年（1462年）九月病歿し、同年十一月、景陵に合葬された。

景陵冬雪

The Triple Gates of Jingling.　Jingling in the Snow

景陵の冬雪

景陵三座门

The Tomb of Jingling

景陵の三座門

景陵陵园前景为祾恩殿基址

Jingling Necropolis
The front view is the foundation of Ling'endian.

景陵の陵園　　前景は祾恩殿の遺跡である。

裕陵

Yuling

裕陵

裕陵葬英宗皇帝朱祁镇。

朱祁镇（公元 1427——1464 年），九岁即皇帝位。正统十四年（公元 1449 年）亲帅六师出征塞北瓦剌部族时，在土木（今河北怀来县境）被也先俘虏，史称"土木之变"。一年后送回北京，但逊位于胞弟朱祁钰，以太上皇名分闲居"南内"。七年后利用"夺门"复辟，重登帝位。天顺八年（公元 1464 年）病逝，年仅三十八岁。

皇后钱氏，与朱祁镇同年生，无子女，成化四年（公元 1468 年）病逝，年四十六岁，合葬裕陵。

皇贵妃周氏，因生皇长子（即宪宗帝）被尊为皇太后，待到皇长孙即位，尊称为太皇太后，弘治十一年（公元 1498 年）病卒，享年七十五岁，与英宗合葬裕陵。一帝二后合葬自裕陵始。

Zhu Qizheng, Emperor Ying Zong was buried in Yuling.

Zhu Qizheng (1427——1464) succeeded to the throne at the age of 9. In 1449 when he personally commanded his army to fight against the Wala tribe of the Monggol nationality, he was arrested in Tumu (present Huailai County, Hebei) which is known as "Tumu Incident" in the Chinese history. A year later, he was sent back to Beijing. But as his brother Zhu Qiyu had already taken his place, he stayed in the palace idle as a backstage ruler. Seven years later, he took over the power and became the emperor again. In 1464, he died of illness when he was only 38.

Empress Qian, born in the same year as her husband Zhu Qizheng, didn't have any children. In 1468 she died of illness when she was 46, and was buried in the same tomb.

Honourable Imperial Concubine Zhou became Empress Dowager after she gave birth to the first son of Emperor Xian Zong. When her grandson became an emperor, she was respectfully addressed Grand Emperor Dowager. In 1498, she died of illness at the age of 75, and was buried with Ying Zong.

So Yuling contains the remains of the Ming Emperor Ying Zong and his two empresses, Qian and Zhou.

裕陵は英宗皇帝朱祁鎮（正統皇帝）のお陵である。

朱祁鎮（1427－1464年）は、九歳で即位した。正統十四年（1449年）自ら六師を引き連れて、北方にある瓦剌民族に遠征した時、土木（今の河北懐柔県内）で、也先という人によって捕われの身となった。歴史上「土木之変」と言われている。一年後北京に送り帰されたが、弟の朱祁鈺（景泰皇帝）に帝位を譲り、太上皇の位で、「南内」にて静かに暮した。七年後「奪門」を利用して、再び帝位についた。天順八年(1464年)、三十八歳で病殁した。

皇后銭氏は、朱祁鎮と同年に生まれ、子供がいない。成化四年（1468年）四十六歳で、病殁し、裕陵に合葬された。

貴妃周氏が長男（憲宗帝）を生んだため、皇皇太后と尊ばれ、長孫が帝位についたあと、太皇太后として尊ばれた。弘治十年年（1498年）七十五歳で病死し、英宗と裕陵に合葬された。一帝二后（一人の皇帝と二人の皇后）の合葬は裕陵から始まったのである。

裕陵
—————
Yuling Necropolis
—————
裕陵

裕陵明楼
—————
Minglou in Yuling
—————
裕陵の明楼

茂陵

Maoling

茂 陵

茂陵,葬宪宗皇帝朱见深。为一帝三后合葬陵。

朱见深（公元 1447——1487 年）,英宗长子,十八岁时即位。在位二十二年。四十一岁时病逝。

合葬后妃分别是:

继后王氏,天顺八年（公元 1464 年）十六岁时册封,正德十三年（公元 1534 年）去世,终年七十岁。

太后纪氏（孝宗生母）,成化十一年（公元 1475 年）病卒,因生皇子追封为淑妃,待到孝宗即位,追尊皇太后,成化二十三年（公元 1487 年）迁葬茂陵。

太后邵氏,初封宸妃,因生皇子三人,进封贵妃,世宗即位,尊为皇太后,嘉靖元年十一月卒。第二年（公元 1523 年）二月以皇后礼仪附葬茂陵玄宫之右。

Maoling is the tomb for Zhu Jianshen, Emperor Xian Zong and his three empresses.

Zhu Jianshen (1447--1487), the first son of Emperor Ying Zong, came to power at the age of 18, and occupied the throne for 22 years. He died of illness when he was 41 years old.

The empresses and imperial concubines buried here are:

His second wife Empress Wang became the empress at the age of 16 in 1464. and died in 1534 when she was 70 years old.

Empress Dowager Ji (the mother of Xiao Zong) died of illness in 1475. She was posthumously granted the title of Imperial Concubine for having given birth to the son of Emperor Xiao Zong, and later the title of Empress Dowager after Xiao Zong succeeded the throne. In 1487 her remains were transferred to Maoling.

Empress Dowager Shao was initially raised to the rank of imperial concubine. Having given birth to 3 sons, she was made Honourable Imperial concubine. When Si Zong came to power, she became Empress Dowager. She died in January 1522. Treated as an empress, a funeral ceremony was held in February of the following year when she was reburied on the right side of Emperor Xian Zong in the underground palace of Maoling.

茂陵には憲宗皇帝朱見深（成化皇帝）が埋葬されていて、一帝三后の合葬陵である。

朱見深（1447～1487年）は、英宗の長男で、十八歳で即位し、二十二年間在位した。四十一歳で病歿。

合葬されている皇后、貴妃は以下の通りである。

後妻王氏は、天順八年（1464年）十六歳で皇后に封ぜられ、正徳十三年（1534年）崩御、享年七十歳。

皇太后紀氏（孝宗の母親）は成化十一年（1475年）病死。皇子を生んだため、死後淑妃に封ぜられ、孝宗が帝位についてから、皇太后と尊ばれ、成化二十三年（1487年）茂陵に改葬された。

皇太后邵氏は、初め宸妃に封ぜられ、皇子三人を生んだため、貴妃に位が上がった。世宗が即位した後、皇太后と尊ばれ、嘉靖元年十一月逝去した。翌年（1323年）二月皇后の儀礼で茂陵玄宮の右に合葬された。

远眺茂陵

Maoling Viewed from the Distance

遠くから眺めた茂陵

茂陵　　前景为祾恩殿遗址

Maoling Necropolis　　The front view
is the ruins of Ling'endian.

茂陵　　前景は祾恩殿の遺跡である。

Tailing

泰　陵

泰陵是孝宗皇帝朱祐樘与皇后张氏的合葬陵。

朱祐樘（公元 1470——1505 年），十八岁时即帝位，据说由于长年服用丹药，致使燥火上升，弘治十八年五月病死于乾清宫，年三十六岁。

皇后张氏，与皇帝同年生，十八岁时册封，嘉靖二十年（公元 1541 年）八月病卒。年七十一岁。同年十一月葬泰陵。

Tailing contains the remains of Zhu Youtang, Emperor Xiao Zong and his wife Empress Zhang.

Zhu Youtang (1470––1505) ascended the throne at the age of 18. He died of illness in Qianqinggong in May 1505 when he was only 36.

His wife Empress Zhang, born in the same year, became the empress when she was 18 years old. She died of illness in August 1541 at the age of 71, and was buried in Tailing in November of the same year.

泰陵は孝宗皇帝朱祐樘（弘治皇帝）と皇后張氏の合葬陵である。

朱祐樘（1470～1505年）は十八歳で即位し、言い伝えによると、長年丹薬（長寿の薬）を服用していたが、副作用の為、弘治十八年五月、三十六歳の時乾清宮で病歿した。

皇后張氏は皇帝と同年に生まれ、十八歳の時皇后に封ぜられ、嘉靖二十年（1541年）八月、七十一歳で病死した。同年十一月泰陵に埋葬された。

泰陵二柱门

The Two-pillar Gate of Tailing

泰陵の二柱門

泰陵明楼

Minglou of Tailing

泰陵の明楼

康　陵

Kangling

康　陵

康陵葬武宗皇帝朱厚熜与皇后夏氏。

朱厚熜（公元 1491——1521 年），十四岁时即帝位，在位十六年。三十一岁时病逝。

皇后夏氏，南京上元人，弘治六年（公元 1493 年）生，十四岁时册封为皇后，嘉靖十四年（公元 1519 年）正月卒，年四十三岁，同年三月葬康陵。

Kangling is the tomb for Zhu Houzhao, Emperor Wu Zong and his wife Empress Xia.

Zhu Houzhao (1491—1521) became emperor at the age of 14 and reigned for 16 years. He died of illness at the age of 31.

His wife Empress Xia was born in Shangyuan County, Nanjing in 1493, and became the empress when she was 14 years old. She died in January 1519 at the age of 26, and was buried in Kangling in March of the same year.

康陵には武宗皇帝朱厚熜（正徳皇帝）と皇后夏氏が埋葬されている。

朱厚熜（正徳皇帝）と皇后夏氏が埋葬されている。

朱厚熜（1491～1521年）は十四歳で即位し、在位十六年、三十一歳で病気で崩御。

皇后夏氏は南京上元の人で、弘治六年（1493年）に生まれ、十四歳の時、皇后に封ぜられ、嘉靖十四年（1519年）正月崩御、享年四十三歳。同年三月康陵に埋葬された。

康陵二柱门

The Two-pillar Gate of Kangling

康陵の二柱門

康陵前景

The Front View of Kangling

康陵の前景

康陵春色

Kangling in Spring

康陵の春色

31

永　陵
Yongling

永　陵

　　永陵,是世宗皇帝朱厚熜生前予建的。始建于嘉靖十五年(公元1536年),世宗亲拟陵寝规制,从用料到施工工艺,不少地方都是长陵所不及的。

　　朱厚熜(公元1507——1566年),宪宗孙,其父兴献王封番湖北安陆(今钟祥县),武宗皇帝无子嗣,朱厚熜以堂弟入京即位。在位四十五年,终年六十岁。

　　合葬永陵的后妃共三人。

　　皇后陈氏,大名府元城人,嘉靖元年册封,七年十月病卒,年仅二十一岁。死后葬陵区西南隅,是为悼灵皇后陵,隆庆元年(公元1567年)迁葬永陵。

　　继后方氏,初封德嫔,嘉靖十三年(公元1534年)册封为后,二十六年卒。因护卫皇帝有功,遂先于世宗入葬永陵。

　　杜太后,大兴人,初为康嫔,卒于嘉靖三十三年(公元1554年),因生皇三子(是为穆宗),于隆庆元年(公元1567年)迁葬永陵。

　　Yongling was constructed in 1536 when Zhu Houzong, Emperor Shi Zong was still alive. Emperor Shi Zong mapped out the programme personally for the tomb. So it is far more magnificent than Changling in many aspects from the materials used to the art of architectural design.

　　Zhu Houzong (1507——1566) was a grandson of Emperor Xian Zong. His father was Prince Xingxian whose feudal estates was Anlu (present Zhong Xiang County), Hubei. As emperor Wu Zong didn't have any sons to succeed to the throne, his cousin Zhu Houzong came to Beijing to take the power. The latter had been the emperor for 45 years and died at the age of 60.

　　Buried together with him were three empresses and concubines.

　　Empress Chen from Yuancheng, Damingfu (present Daming County, Hebei), became the empress in 1522 and died in October 1528 at the age of 21. She was buried in a tomb reserved for imperial concubines in the southwest corner of the necropolis. In 1567 her remains were transferred to the tomb of Yongling.

　　The second Empress Fang who was first raised to the rank of concubine became the empress in 1534, and die in 1547. As she had made contributions to pretecting the emperor, she was buried in Yongling prior to Emperor Shi Zong.

　　Empress Dowager Du From Daxing (present Daxing County in Beijing) was initially made a concubine. She died in 1554. As she had given birth to the Emperor's third son who later became Emperor Mu Zong, her remains were transferred to Yongling in 1567.

　　永陵は世宗皇帝朱厚熜(嘉靖皇帝)の生前に造営されたもので、嘉靖十五年(1536年)造営し始めたものである。世宗が自ら陵寝の造営に携わった永陵の材料や工事の技術は長陵のそれを凌いでいる。

　　朱厚熜(1507～1566年)は憲宗の孫で、父親の興献王が、湖北安陸(今の鍾祥県)藩の藩主であった。武宗皇帝にあととり息子がいないため、いとこの朱厚熜が都に入り、即位した。

　　永陵に合葬されたのは后妃の三人である。

　　皇后陳氏は大名府元城の人で、嘉靖元年皇后に封ぜられ、七年十月、二十一歳で病没。死後、皇后陵を悼むため、陵区西南隅に埋葬され、隆慶元年(1567年)永陵に改葬された。

　　後妻方氏は、初め徳嬪に封ぜられ、嘉靖十三年(1534年)皇后に封ぜられた。二十六年崩御。皇帝を守り、手柄を立てたため、世宗が永陵に入る前に埋葬された。

　　杜太后は、大興の人で、初め康嬪であった。三十三年に逝去。皇三子(穆宗皇帝)を生んだため、隆慶元年(1567年)永陵に改葬された。

永陵全景　前为祾恩门基址

Full View of Yongling　The front view is the foundation of Ling'enmen (Gate of Prominent Favour).

永陵の全景　前は祾恩門の遺跡である。

永陵丹陛　永陵祾恩殿之丹陛石,雕有"龙凤呈祥"纹饰。

A Flight of Steps Leading to Ling's endian of Yongling　The ornamental centre–piece of stone steps are carved with long (Chinese dragon) and feng (phoenix) design.

永陵の丹陛　永陵祾恩殿の丹陛石で、「龍鳳呈祥」の模様が彫られている。

永陵瑞雪　明楼之斗拱构件全用石料雕琢制作,结构严谨,至今完好如初。

Yongling in the Snow　Built completely of stone and brick, Minglou serves as a landmark for the entire tomb. It is strong in structure, with brackets carved out of stone inserted between a culumn and a crossbeam. It is still in good condition with no damage from erosion by rain and wind in the past four hundred years.

永陵の瑞雪　明楼の斗拱部材はすべて石を彫って作られている。組み立て方もしっかりしており、今日まで完全な形で現存されている。

昭陵

Zhaoling

昭陵

昭陵，葬穆宗皇帝朱载垕，为一帝三后合葬陵。

朱载垕（公元 1537——1572 年），世宗第三子，初封裕王，三十岁时即帝位，在位六年，终年三十六岁。

追赠后李氏，嘉靖三十一年（公元 1522 年）册封为裕王妃，三十七年病卒。原葬西山丰裕口，朱载垕即位，追赠为皇后，神宗即位，迁葬昭陵。

皇后陈氏，北通州（今通县）人，初为裕王继妃，后册封为皇后，万历三十四年（公元 1606 年）卒于慈庆宫，同年葬昭陵。

进称后李氏，嘉靖二十四年（公元 1545 年）生，神宗皇帝生母，万历四十二年（公元 1614 年）卒于慈宁宫，终年七十岁，附葬昭陵。

Zhaoling is the tomb for Zhu Zaihou, Emperor Mu Zong and his three empresses.

Zhu Zaihou (1537--1572), the third son of Emperor Shi Zong, was initially made Prince Yu. When he was 30 years old, he ascended the throne and reigned for 6 years. He was only 36 years old when he died.

Madame Li, who was posthumously granted the title of empress after Zhu Zaihou came to power, became Princes Yu in 1522. She died of illness 6 years later and was buried in Fengyukou, Xishan (present Fragrance Hill). When Shen Zong was the emperor, her remains were transferred to Zhaoling.

Empress Chen from Beitong Zhou (present Tongxian County, Beijing) was first promoted to be the second concubine of Prince Yu and later became the empress. She died in Ciqingong in 1606 and was buried in Zhaoling in the same year.

Born in 1545, Empress Li was the mother of Emperor Shen Zong. She died in Cininggong in 1614 at the age of 70, and was buried in Zhaoling.

昭陵は、穆宗皇帝朱載垕（隆慶皇帝）のお陵で、一帝三后の合葬陵である。

朱載垕（1537～1572年）は、世宗の第三子で、初め裕王に封ぜられ、三十歳の時即位した。在位六年、享年三十六歳。

追贈皇后陳氏は嘉靖三十一年（1522年）裕王妃に封ぜられ、三十七年病歿。もともと西山豊裕口に埋葬されたが、朱載垕が即位した後、皇后に追贈された。神宗が即位して、昭陵に改葬された。

皇后陳氏は、北通州（今の通県）の人で、初め裕王継妃であったが、後ちに皇后に封ぜられ、万暦三十四年（1606年）慈慶宮で崩御。同年昭陵に埋葬された。

進称皇后李氏は、嘉靖三十四年（1545年）に生まれ、神宗皇帝の母親で、万暦四十二年（1614年）、七十歳で慈寧宮で崩御し、昭陵に合葬された。

雪映昭陵

Zhaoling in the Snow

雪の光に映える昭陵

装饰一新的稜恩门

Newly-decorated Ling'endian

新しく装飾された稜恩門

昭陵全景

Full View of Zhaoling

昭陵の全景

棂星门

Lattice Gate（LingXing Men）

櫺星門

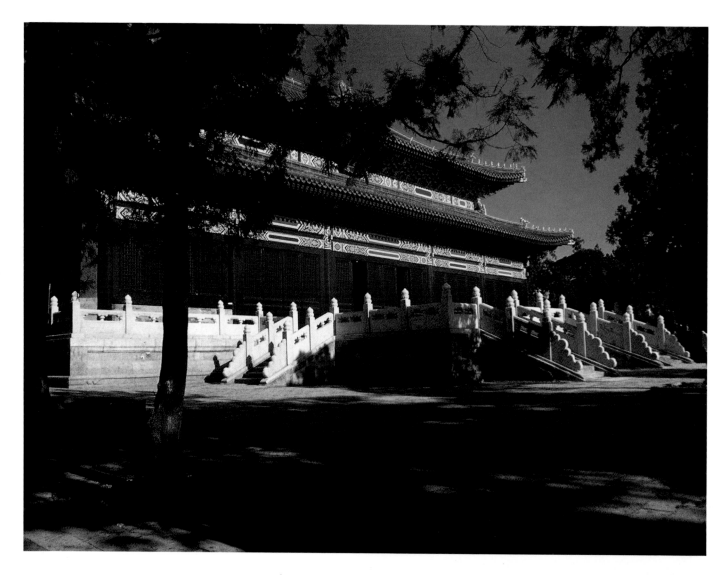

昭陵棱恩殿　　昭陵棱恩殿在康熙年间毁于雷火，后曾重建，亦无存。现建筑为近年在原墓址上重建的。

Ling'endian in Zhaoling　　It was destroyed in the fire during the Kangxi period of Qing Dynasty. Later it was rebuilt but destroyed again. The present structure you have seen was rebuilt in recent years on the original site of the tomb.

昭陵の棱恩殿　　昭陵の棱恩殿は、清康熙年間、雷で焼失した。その後再建されたが、今はもう残っていない。今の建物は近年元の墓の場所で建て直された物である。

棱恩殿内三牲祭祀原状陈列

Three sacrificial animals are in the original sacrificing state on display in Ling'endian

棱恩殿内の三牲祭祀が元の状態のまま陳列されている。

桃花映昭陵

Zhaoling amid the Peach Blossom

桃の花に映える昭陵

穆宗皇帝像　　近年来，对昭陵进行了修缮，并在陵内设置了一帝三后的史料陈列。穆宗像 是根据《历代帝后像》资料复原制作的。

Portrait of Emperor Muzong　　In recent years, Zhaoling has been renovated, and the historical data for the emperor and his three empresses are on display in the exhibition room of the tomb. The portrait of Muzong is painted based on the *Portraits of Emperors and Empresses of Past Ages*.

穆宗皇帝像　　近年来、昭陵に対して修理が行なわれていた。そして、陵内にて一帝二后の史料が陳列されている。穆宗の肖像画は「歴代帝后像」の資料から復原して、作られたものである。

Dingling

定　陵

　　定陵是神宗皇帝朱翊钧生前予建的。因执意仿永陵建造，所以规模宏大，施工精细，始建于万历十二年（公元 1584 年），历时六年，耗银八百万两。

　　朱翊钧（公元 1563——1620 年），十岁即帝位，在位四十八年。

　　与其合葬的有：

　　孝端后王氏，浙江余姚人，嘉靖四十三年（公元 1564 年）生，不足十五岁时册封为后，万历四十八年（公元 1620 年）四月病卒。年五十七岁。与朱翊钧同期葬定陵。

　　孝靖后王氏，嘉靖四十四年（公元 1565 年）生，十四岁入宫，万历十年（公元 1582 年）生皇长子（光宗皇帝），封王氏为恭妃。三十九年（公元 1611 年）四十七岁时病逝。初葬陵区内平岗地，皇长孙即位，于万历四十八年（公元 1620 年）十月迁葬定陵。

　　Dingling was built when Zhu Yijun, Emperor Shen Zong was still alive. As he insisted on building his tomb similar to Yongling, the construction was great in scale. Starting in 1584, it took 6 years to complete, at the cost of eight million taels of silver.

　　Zhu Yijun (1563--1620) ascended the throne at the age of 10 and ruled 48 years until he died in 1620.

　　His two wives were also buried here together with him. They are:

　　His second wife Empress Xiaojing, born in 1565, came to the palace at the age of 14. She was promoted to the rank of imperial concubine in 1582 when she had the first son of Emperor Guang Zong. In 1611 she died of illness when she was 47 years old. As the second wife, she was not entitled to the privilege of sharing the Emperor's tomb. So she was first buired in a nearby tomb in Pinggangdi. After her grandson came to power, she was raised posthumously to the rank of Empress Dowager, and her remains were moved into the tomb in October 1620.

　　定陵は神宗皇帝朱翊鈞（万暦皇帝）が生前造営されたものである。

　　我を張って永陵に真似て造営したので、規模が大きく、細かいところまで工夫が凝らされている。万暦十二年から、造営に六年の歳月をかけ、銀八百万両（一両＝50グラム）を費した。

　　朱翊鈞（1563～1620年）は、わずか十歳で即位し、在位四十八年。

　　神宗皇帝と合葬されたのは、孝端皇后と孝靖皇后である。

　　孝端皇后王氏は、浙江余姚の出身で、嘉靖四十四年（1564年）に生まれ、十五歳足らずで皇后に封ぜられ、万暦四十八年（1620年）四月に病殁した。享年五十八歳。朱翊鈞と同じ時期に定陵に埋葬された。

　　孝靖皇后王氏は、嘉靖四十四年（1565年）に生まれ、十四歳で入宮し、万暦十年（1582年）長男（光宗皇帝）を生んだため、恭妃に封ぜられた。三十九年（1611年）四十七歳の時、病殁した。初め陵区内の平岗地に埋葬されれたが、長孫が皇帝に即位し、万暦四十八年（1620年）十月、定陵に改葬された。

定陵陵门

The Gate of Dingling

定陵の陵門

定陵陵园

Dingling Necropolis

定陵の陵園

定陵无字碑

Stele Without Inscription in Dingling

定陵の無字碑

定陵明楼

Minglou in Dingling

定陵の明楼

定陵鸟瞰

A Bird's Eye View of Dingling

定陵の鳥瞰図

万历帝画像

The Portrait of Emperor Wanli

万暦皇帝の肖像画

孝靖后画像

The Portrait of Empress Xiaojing

孝靖后の肖像画

孝端后画像

The Portrait of Empress Xiaoduan

孝靖皇后の肖像画

地宮入口

The entrance to the Underground Palace

地宮の入口

地下宮殿出入口

The exit of the Underground Palace

地下宮殿の出入り口

金刚墙

Diamond Wall

金剛壁

地宫后殿　后殿是玄宫的主要部分,停放着一帝二后的棺椁及陪葬器物、箱子,地面铺的花斑石。地面至券顶高9.5米,南北长30多米,宽9米,全部巨石叠砌。

The Rear Chamber of the Underground Palace　Being the main section of the Underground Palace, the rear chamber is the place where the coffins of Emperor Wan Li and his two expresses are placed along with burial objects and chests. Built entirely of huge rocks, the chamber is over 30 metres long, 9.1 metres wide and 9.5 metres high. The floor is paved with polished porphyritic rocks.

地宮の後殿　後殿は玄宮の主な部分で、一帝二后の棺椁、及び副葬品、木箱などが置かれていた。地面に敷いてあるのは花斑石である。地面から天井までの高さは9.5mで、南北の長さ30m余り、広さ9mである。全部巨大石で積み重ねて、作られている。

地宮中殿

Middle Chamber in the Underground Palace

地宮中殿

地下玄宮中殿

Middle Chamber of the Underground Palace

地下玄宮中殿

配殿　　以对称格局建造的左、右两配殿规格相同，东西长 26 米，南北宽 7 米，地面至券顶 7.4 米，有棺床，但在发掘时，发现棺床上并未放置任何物品。

Peidian (Annex Chambers)　　The left and right Peidian are two symmetrical structures. Each is 26 metres long from east to west, 7 metres wide from north to south and 7.4 metres high with its walls rising in an arch to the ceiling. In the middle of each chamber is a coffin platform on which no objects were found when it was excavated.

　　配殿　　左右対称という構造で作られた二つの配殿の規格は同じで、東西の長さ26ｍ、南北の広さ７ｍ、地面から天井までの高さは、7.4ｍである。中には棺床（棺椁を置くための台）が造ってあるが、その上に何も置かれていなかった。

Treasures in Dingling

定 陵 の 宝 物

　　为开展历史研究，经报请国务院批准，一九五六年五月正式发掘了定陵。历时一年，终于找到并打开了进入地下玄宫的金刚墙。

　　定陵先后出土了各类文物三千余件。其中以帝后生前宫中使用的金、银、玉、瓷器，以及冠服、饰物居多。可谓品类齐全，制作精美。不少文物的制作反映了当时的最高工艺水平。具有一定的史料及科研价值。

　　Approved by the State Council, the excavation of Dingling started in May 1956. It took one year to uncover and open the Diamond Wall of the Underground Palace.

　　About 3,000 burial objects were unearthed in Dingling, and many were articles of gold, silver, jade and porcelain for daily use by the emperor and empresses in the imperial palace. There were also imperial robes and decorative objects which were beautifully made. Many of the excavated objects really reflect the highest level of technology and workmanship at that time, valuable for the scientific research.

　　歴史の研究を推し推めるため、国務院の認可により、一九五六年五月、正式に定陵の発掘を始めた。一年かかって、ついに地下玄宮に入る金剛壁を発見した。

　　定陵から、各種類の文物三千個余りが出土された。そのうち、皇帝と皇后の生前宮中で使われていた金、銀、玉、磁器及び衣冠、装飾品が多くを占めている。それらは精密で、種類も多く、美しいものである。

"岁岁平安"金耳坠

Gold Eardrop of safe and sound Years

「歳歳平安」金耳墜（耳飾り）

三龙三凤冠

Crown with Three Dragons and Three Phoenixes

三龍三鳳冠

金托盖白玉碗

White Jade Bowl

金托蓋白玉碗

玉壶
————
Jade pot
————
玉壺

三彩瓷炉

The Tri-colour Incense Burner

三彩磁炉

金爵

Gold Wine Vessel

金爵

青花大龙缸

Huge Jar with Dragon Designs

青花大龍甕

金"八宝"革带

Gold Belt of Eight Treasures

金「八宝」革带

顶簪

Hairpin for the Crown of the Head

頂簪

龙首玉如意带钩

S-shaped Ornamental Jade Hook

龍首玉如意鈎

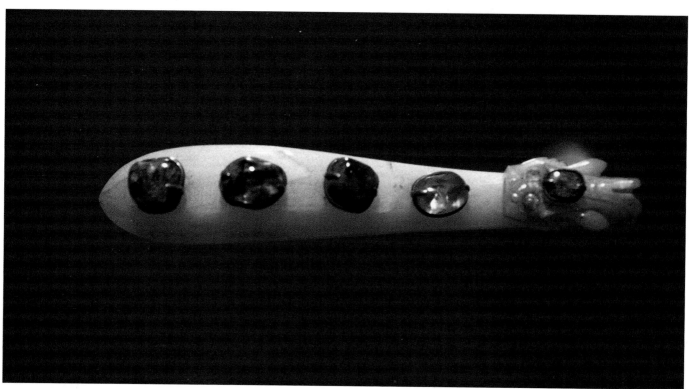

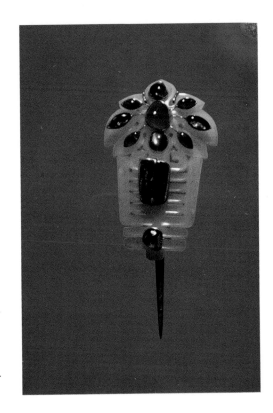

金簪

Gold Hairpin

金簪

寿字金簪

Gold Hairpin with
the Character of
Longevity

寿字金簪

玉寿字金耳坠

Gold Eardrop with a Jade Character of Longevity

玉寿金字耳墜（耳飾り）

缂丝十二章衮服（复制品）

**Emperor's Silk Ceremonial Costume
with Dragon, Sun and Moon Designs**

緙絲十二章毛皮の衣

冕
——
Crown
——
冕

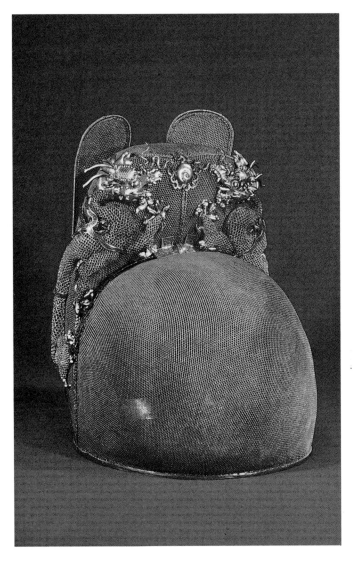

金丝翼善冠

Emperor Wanli's Gold Headdress with Gold Mesah Head Support

金絲翼善冠

乌纱翼善冠

Gold Headdress with Black Chiffon Head Support

烏紗翼善冠

刺绣百子衣（复制品）

Embroidered Robe with the "Hundred Boys" Pattern

刺繡の百子衣

慶陵

Qingling

慶陵

庆陵，葬光宗皇帝朱常洛及其后妃，为四人合葬陵。

朱常洛（公元 1582——1620 年），神宗长子，十九岁时立为皇太子，万历四十八年七月父皇神宗去世，朱常洛即位，仅一个月，便因病卒于乾清宫，年三十八岁。

孝元皇后郭氏，顺天府人，万历三十年（公元 1602 年）与十九岁的皇太子成婚，四十一年病卒，天启元年（公元 1621 年）迁葬庆陵。

孝和皇后王氏，因生皇长子（后为熹宗皇帝）封为才人，万历四十七年（公元 1619 年）三月病卒，熹宗即位。于天启元年（公元 1621 年）以皇后礼迁葬庆陵。

孝纯皇后刘氏，宛平人，生于万历二十年（公元 1592 年）初入宫为淑女，万历三十八年（公元 1610 年）生皇五子（即崇祯皇帝），四十二年郁疾而卒，年仅二十三岁。崇祯帝即位，以皇后礼迁葬庆陵。

Qingling contains the remains of Zhu Changluo, Emperor Guang Zong and his 3 expresses.

Zhu Changluo (1582—1620), the eldest son of Emperor Shen Zong was chosen Crown Prince when he was 19 years old. When his father Emperor Shen Zong died in 1620, he succeeded him to the throne and remained in power for only one month. He died of illness in Qianqinggong at the age of 38.

Originally from Shuntianfu (present Beijing), Madame Guo was married to the Crown Prince in 1602 when she was 19 years old and later granted the title of Empress Xiaoyuan when Zhu Changluo became the emperor. She died of illness in 1613 and her remains were moved to the tomb in 1621.

Madame Wang, Empress Xiaohe was initially named gifted scholar after giving birth to the first son who later became Emperor. She died of illness in 1619. She was given a funeral ceremony for an empress when her remains were transferred to Qingling in 1621 after her son ascended the throne.

Madame Liu, titled Empress Xiaochun, was born in Wanping (present an area in Lugouqiao) in 1592. She was a maiden at first serving in the imperial palace. In 1610 she had the fifth son who later became the last Ming Emperor Chong Zhen. She died of illness in 1614. When her son succeeded to the throne and became the emperor, her body was moved to the tomb.

慶陵は光宗皇帝朱常洛（泰昌皇帝）とその后妃が埋葬されているところで、四人の合葬陵である。

朱常洛（1582～1620年）は、神宗の長男で、十九歳時の、皇太子に封ぜられ、万暦四十八年七月、父親の神宗が崩御し、朱常洛が即位した。わずか一ヶ月在位し、三十八歳で、乾清宮で病歿した。

孝元皇后郭氏は、順天府の人で、万暦三十年（1602年）、十九歳の皇太子と結婚し、四十一年に病歿した。天啓元年（1621年）慶陵に改葬された。

孝和皇后王氏は、皇長男（熹宗皇帝）を生んだため、才人に封ぜられ、万暦四十七年（1619年）三月病歿。熹宗が即位した後、天啓元年（1621年）皇后の儀礼にて、慶陵に改葬された。

孝純皇后劉氏は、宛平の人で、万暦二十年（1592年）に生まれ、入宮したばかりの頃淑女であったが、万暦三十八年（1610年）、皇第五子（即ち崇禎皇帝）を生んだ。その後四十二年憂うつ病で亡くなった。崇禎皇帝が即位してから、皇后の儀礼で、慶陵に改葬された。

庆陵 前为祾恩殿遗址，后为明楼。

Qingling Necropolis The front view is the ruins of Ling'endian, and the rear view is Minglou (Soul Tower).

慶陵 前は祾恩殿の遺跡で、後ろは明楼である。

庆陵远景

Qingling Viewed from the Distance

慶陵の遠景

庆陵三座门

Triple Gates in Qingling

慶陵の三座門

德陵

Deling

德　陵

德陵。葬熹宗皇帝朱由校与皇后张氏。

朱由校（公元 1605——1627 年），光宗第一子，十五岁时即帝位。在位七年，病卒时年仅二十三岁。

皇后张氏，天启元年（公元 1621 年）与十六岁的皇帝行大婚礼。公元 1644 年李自成进京，皇后自缢身亡。同年五月合葬德陵。

Deling is the tomb for Zhu Youxiao, Emperor Xi Zong and his wife Empress Zhang.

Being the first son of Emperor Guang Zong, Zhu Youxian (1605——1627) ascended the throne at the age of 15, whose reign lasted for 7 years. He died of illness when he was 23 years old.

His wife Empress Zhang was married to him at the age of 16 in 1621. She hanged herself in 1644 when Li Zicheng, the leader of the peasant insurrectionary army broke into Beijing, and was buried in the tomb with the emperor in May of the same year.

德陵は、熹宗皇帝朱由校（天啓皇帝）と皇后張氏が埋葬されているところである。

朱由校（1605～1627年）は、光宗の長男で、十五歳で即位し、在位七年。二十三歳の時病歿した。

皇后張氏は、天啓元年（1621年）十六歳の皇帝と結婚した。1644年李自成が北京に入ったため、皇后が首を吊って自殺した。同年五月德陵に改葬された。

德陵二柱门及明楼

The Two-pillar Gate and Minglou in Deling

德陵の二柱門と明楼

德陵神宫监　明朝皇帝陵寝由宫中派出的太监主持洒扫事宜,并举行正朔祭祀等活动,神宫监是太监的住所及管理机构之所在。

Holy Imperial Office in Deling.　The Tombs of the Ming Dynasty emperors were swept and managed by the eunches from the palace. It is the place where sacrifices were held on the luner New Year's Day. The Holy Imperial office was the eunuches' living quarters as well as the administrative office.

德陵の神宮監　明朝皇帝の陵寝は、宮中から派遣された太監によって、掃除と管理をされていた。それに、正朔祭祀の行事も太監によって行なわれていた。神宮監というのは太監の住むところと管理機関の所在地である。

德陵春色

Deling in Spring

德陵の春色

徳陵全景

Full View of Deling

徳陵の全景

思陵

Siling

思　陵

思陵葬崇祯帝朱由检，为一帝二后妃合葬墓。

朱由检（公元 1610——1644 年），光宗第五子，天启二年（公元 1622 年）封为信王，七年（公元 1627 年）以"兄终弟及"的祖训即皇帝位。时年十七岁。崇祯十七年（公元 1644 年）三月，李自成进京，朱由检自缢煤山，后来由义军办理丧事，葬朱由检于陵区西南隅的田贵妃坟园。

周皇后，初为信王妃，后进封皇后，崇祯十七年义军攻入北京，周氏自缢身亡，与朱由检同期入葬田贵妃坟园。

田贵妃，入宫后甚得宠幸，崇祯元年（公元 1628 年）册封为贵妃，十五年病逝。在陵区内鹿马山前建坟园，十七年正月入葬，两个月后崇祯帝后亦合葬于此，是为思陵。

Siling is the tomb for Zhu Youjian, Emperor Chong Zhen and his two empresses.

Zhu Youjian (1610—1644), the fifth son of Emperor Guang Zong, was made Prince Xin in 1622. As his brother Emperor Xi Zong didn't have any sons to succeed him to the throne, Zhu Youjian became the emperor, according to the rule set by their ancestors when Emperor Xi Zong died in 1627. He was only 17 years old at that time. He hanged himself on the Coal Hill in 1644 when Li Zicheng led the peasant army to Beijing. His funeral was held by the peasant army and buried in the tomb of Honourable Imperial Concubine Tian in the southwest corner of the imperial cemetery.

His wife Empress Zhou was first promoted to Princess Xin and later became the empress. She hanged herself in 1644 when the peasant army led by Li Zicheng broke into Beijing. She was buried together with Emperor Zhu Youjian in the tomb of Honourable Imperial Concubine Tian.

Honourable Imperial Concubine Tian was the emperor's beloved concubine who was promoted to be the highest-ranking imperial concubine in 1628. She died of illness in 1642. A tomb was built for her in the southwest of the necropolis, and she was buried in it in January 1644, two month prior to Emperor Chong Zhen and Empress Zhou. It was named Siling when the emperor and the empress were buried here.

思陵は、崇禎皇帝朱由検が埋葬されているところで、一帝二后妃の合葬陵である。

朱由検（1610～1644年）は、光宗の第五子で、天啓二年（1622年）、信王に封ぜられ、七年（1627年）「兄終弟及」という父祖の教訓で、帝位についた。当時十七歳であった。崇禎十七年（1644年）三月、李自成が北京に入ったため、朱由検は煤山で首を吊って自殺した。その後、義兵によって葬式が行なわれ、朱由検を陵区西南隅の田貴妃墓地に埋葬された。

周皇后は、初め信王妃であったが、その後皇后に封せられた。崇禎七年、義兵が北京に入ったため、周氏が首を吊って自殺した。周皇后は朱由検と同じ時期に田貴妃墓地に埋葬されている。

田貴妃は入宮してから、大変寵愛されて、崇禎元年（1628年）貴妃に封ぜられた。十五年、病歿した。陵区内の鹿馬山の前に墓地を造営し、十七年正月、その中に埋葬された。その二ヶ月後には、崇禎皇帝と皇后も合葬された。それが思陵である。

石香炉

Stone Incense burner

石香炉

王承恩墓 崇祯帝自缢煤山,满朝文武大都逃散,只有太监王承恩追随其后,在崇祯帝身边自缢身亡。清军入关,遂将他葬在思陵右侧。

Wang Chengen's Grave. Being Pursued by the peasant army led by Li Zicheng, all the civil and military officials ran away except Wang Chengen who followed Emperor Chong Zhen closely. The Emperor hanged himself on an old locust tree on Coal Hill and Wang Chengen hanged himself on a tree next to him. Later, he was buried on the right side of Siling.

王承恩のお墓 崇禎皇帝が煤山で首吊り自殺した後、朝廷の文武官は皆逃げてしまったが、太監王承恩だけが残り、後を追うように崇禎皇帝のそばで首を吊って自殺した。そして、清軍が北京に入り、彼を思陵の右側に埋葬した。

思陵圣号碑

Shenghao Stele of Siling

思陵の聖号碑

天寿山　　　　　　　　　　　　　　陽翠岭

庆陵　献陵　　长陵　　　景陵　永陵　　德陵

　　　　　　　　　　　　　　　　东井

　　　七孔桥　　　行宫　　　工部厂

　　　　　　　　　　　　　　　　　　内监公署

行宫　　　　龙凤门

神路　　　　　　　　　　　　　　长陵园

感恩殿(行宫)

围墙　　　　　　　　　龙山

十三陵示意图

Sketch Map of the Ming Tombs

十三陵の案内図

67

（京）新登字 031 号

编　　委：李学东　杨　茵　吴建群
摄　　影：朱　力　张肇基　杨　茵　王文波　魏玉清
撰　　稿：魏玉清
翻　　译：朱小琴　周　莉
责任编辑：李新美
设计装帧：武　悦
技术编辑：柳景林

Editorial Board：Li Xuedong Yang Yin Wu Jianqun
Photographers：Zhu Li Zhang Zhaoji Yang Yin Wang Wenbo Wei Yuqing
Composer：Wei Yuqing
Translators：Zhu Xiaoqin　Zhou Li
Editor in Charge：Li Xin Mei
Art Designer：Wu Yue
Technical Editor：Liu Jinglin

編集：李学東　杨茵　吴建群
摄影：朱力　張肇基　杨茵　王文波　**魏玉清**
撰稿：魏玉清
翻訳：朱小琴　周莉
責任編輯：李新美
イラスト編集：武悦
技術編集：柳景林